Conten

Tiger, Tiger

Written by Judy Ling

3

teeth

Tigers have teeth.

jaws

Tigers have jaws.

whiskers

Tigers have whiskers.

paws

Tigers have paws.

stripes

Tigers have stripes.

claws

Tigers have claws.

And tigers have very scary...

roars!

13

Jellybean Is Lost

Written by Wendy Blaxland
Illustrated by Jennifer Cooper

We look in the garden.

No Jellybean!

We look
up the tree.

No Jellybean!

We look under the house.

No Jellybean!

We look on the bed.

No Jellybean!

16 We look in the cupboard.

Lots of
Jellybeans!

17

A poem to share

Kangaroo
Kicks

Kenny Kangaroo
is a keen ball player.
When it comes to kicking,
he is king for the day.
He kicks to Koala
and he kicks to Kitten,
then he kicks the ball
past the keeper – *HOORAY!*

K k K k K k K k K k K

Stretchy Cat

Written by Sue Butcher

Illustrated by Angela Harland and Andrew Leck

25

Stretchy cat is hungry.

He stretches up for cat food.

He stretches up for fish.

He stretches up for sausages.

Stretchy cat is not hungry.

He stretches out to sleep!

31

Big Cats, Little Cat

Big cats, big cats, can you **purr?**

Cat Splat!

cat

mat

cat

rat

Letters I Know

Jj Kk  Tt

Sounds I Know

 -at

Words I Know

for	he	in	look	up
have	I	is	no	we